MARKETING YOUR INVENTION TO MANUFACTURERS

Protecting and selling your invention

By

Arnold K. Winkelman

Author's note: This book was originally published under the title of The Inventors Guide To Marketing in 1994. This version has been updated and revised.

ISBN: 1-4107-5484-7 (e-book)
ISBN: 1-4107-5483-9 (Paperback)

This book is printed on acid free paper.

1stBooks - rev. 06/18/03

This book is dedicated to my wife, Florence; my sons Keith and Read who have constantly challenged, encouraged, and supported my endeavors. Without their help and belief in me and in what I wanted and needed to do, this book would not have come into being.

INTRODUCTION

The written body of material surrounding inventions, inventors, marketing and promotional companies, patents, patent searches, patent attorneys, and stories about how inventors had their inventions stolen is large and available. The story of the process of marketing an invention, for bringing it from idea to product is a much more lean body of information. Much that is available simply does not tell the inventor how to accomplish the progressive steps from idea to product on the shelf or it is not up to date. Almost 20 years ago I wrote such a book. This is a rewriting of much of that information, an updating of it and some new information taking in the changes of the last 20 years.

I have yet to invent the thing that will make me a successful inventor but I never claimed to be an inventor. What I do know about is marketing, that has been my career. I have applied my knowledge to several different fields including inventing. What I know, what I have learned and what I have learned since I wrote my first invention marketing book is recorded here. I have endeavored to put it into a form that will be usable to the amateur or first time inventor. This, then, is intended as a guide for the person who is making their first attempt at marketing their invention or the person who has not previously had success in marketing their invention. I will start with the idea in your head because it is necessary to lay the foundation in order to protect your ownership. To do that, we will start by defining an inventor.

TABLE OF CONTENTS

Part I DEFINITIONS

The definition of an inventor

An inventor may be anyone who has an idea for a new and useful product or process; or who imagines or envisions a new and useful product or process. Inventors are "idea" people. They are oriented to configure their "ideas" to create new and useful products or processes. I continue to use the words "new and useful" because that is how the U S Patent Office defines what is patentable.

Sometimes inventors become inventors because they work for large companies doing research in well-budgeted development departments. Sometimes they work alone. Sometimes they are highly educated people with degrees in their field. Sometimes they are just people who have a better idea for a product that would solve a problem or that would make life easier. The Lemuelson Center, located in the Smithsonian in Washington, DC, collects information about inventors, how they came to invent a product, and information about the product itself. They do not have much information about how these products were marketed or about any kind of marketing process. I think that they are remiss in not recording the details of how the products in which they are interested were marketed. I would like to see the commonality of the marketing process of these various products.

To be called an "inventor" is an after the fact title. Once you have invented, you are an inventor. However, you will need to market that invention successfully to be recognized as an inventor.

What is an invention?

Every invention begins with an idea in your head. By itself an idea cannot be called an invention. In order to qualify as an invention it must conform to the U S Patent and Trademark Office's definition of a patent; i.e. an idea must be developed into a product, process or design that (1) is new, and (2) is useful.

"Newness" may include the result of bringing together parts, which have already been invented. "Newness" may also include the new use of a previously established process. The make-up mirror is an example. It combined the mirror with florescent light bulbs. While the parts were not new, combining them resulted in a new and useful product that was a patentable invention.

As far as patentability is concerned "new and useful" will suffice. As we explore the vital concept of marketability, our definition will have to expand. An invention that is patentable is not necessarily marketable. The converse is also true. An invention that is not patentable is not necessarily unmaketable. The original hula-hoop, a circular tube of plastic, was not patentable but it was certainly marketable. Later, when Whamo, the manufacturer, added a ball or bell to the inside of the tube, it was patentable.

Part II-PAPERWORK

The importance of keeping records

Imagine the inventors of the wheel, the spear, and the axe. They probably weren't too concerned about protecting their creations or making a profit. Indeed, it probably didn't occur to them that they could "protect" their "ownership" or that they could make a "profit" from them. Their "profit" was being able to carry things, kill animals for food and clothing, and cut, chop and scrape more easily. They weren't concerned about others copying their idea. Others did copy the ideas quite freely as civilization continued to develop. Sometime during the middle Ages, England's reigning monarchs began granting exclusive rights to carry on a specific trade and the patent or Letters Patent was born.

Accompanying the birth of this concept of exclusivity was an emotion that plagues the inventor to this day – paranoia. While the fear that someone may steal one's creation can sometimes approach the irrational, the inventor's fears are often quite justifiable. Inventions have been and can be usurped. Inventors have been and can be cheated – even by reputable companies. An inventor is entitled to his secretive manner and mistrustful emotion, especially when his invention represents a potential fortune that he can realize only by being the first to bring it to the marketplace. Sometimes, however, to be first is impossible. It surprises many people but occasionally more than one person will invent the same or a similar thing at about the same time. Therefore, in order to protect a creation from being either innocently usurped or intentionally stolen, an inventor must follow certain specific procedures.

The inventor's notebook

Since every invention starts as an ides, it is imperative that the idea be recorded. Proper documentation begins with a notebook. The first person to document an idea is the one able to claim rights provided that they continue to work the idea. That means that they must develop and test the idea or hire someone to do it for them. They must also produce and market the idea once it is developed into an invention or it may be considered to be abandoned. One cannot simply write down an idea and claim it as their exclusive property forever.

The best kind of notebook to use is a bound, blank book available at any stationery store. The binding is important. It should be sewn so that pages can be neither inserted or removed without leaving evidence.

On the first page, the inventor should sign their name, address and the date. It is a good practice to have this first page notarized, establishing that the signature and the notebook belong to the inventor. You may also wish to number the pages.

Use the notebook to document every idea and each development or change as soon as they are thought of. Date each entry. Initial or sign each page. Make all entries in ink. NEVER, NEVER ERASE ANYTHING. To make a correction draw a single line through the mistake so that it can still be read. Do not blot out the error. Then correct the mistake. Do not go back and change or revise earlier entries. Instead, make a new entry detailing the changes and dating the change.

Describe your invention clearly. Do not use codes or symbols, which have to be translated. Tell what the invention is, what it does or is supposed to do, how it accomplishes it purpose and how it could be made i.e. The whatsit could be made of plastic using injection molding; or The whatsit could be made of steel and assembled by soldering and using screws and nuts which are readily available or "off the shelf."

Your notebook will become a sequential record of your ideas and their development, much like a diary. Each time you test an idea, make an adjustment, conclude a failure, or succeed with an improvement, you should note the date and describe what you have done and how you've done it. If you hire a person or company to test or produce a part, be sure that you keep all the records including, contract, costs, resulting reports, whatever.

If you never need a paper record such as this, it will never matter but if you do need such a record, you will not be able to go back in time to produce it. It can be invaluable. It has been for many inventors.

Use of Witnesses

Witnesses serve an important purpose. Then lend credibility to your records. Periodically, have at least two witnesses review your notebook and enter their signature and the date. Have them preface their signatures with the statement "Read and understood by," and then sign each time they review your Inventors Notebook. Make sure your witnesses actually do understand your idea and how you intend it to function. They don't have to agree that it will function the way you say it will but they must understand what you have written.

Choose your witnesses with care, keeping in mind that they are to serve as enhancers of your credibility. Select those who have earned a reputation for honesty and are recognized in the community as upstanding. It can be advantageous to have witnesses with technical knowledge in the field of your invention but it is not necessary. Since it could be years, even decades before you might have to call upon your witnesses, consider their age and physical well being as relevant factors. Finally, it is wise to avoid relatives. Their relationship to the inventor, regardless of how distant, considerably weakens their credibility. Remember that you may never need them but if you do, you want them to be the most credible possible.

Record and Disclosure of Invention Form

There are several ways to establish ownership of an idea. None of them is the "right" or "only" way. I recommend using each of the three ways since each has different characteristics. The notebook is a witnessed record of your ideas. The Record and Disclosure of Invention Form is a simple form that is also witnessed and then sent to your own address through the U. S. Mail to confirm the date of the contents. The Disclosure Document Form is a procedure created by the U. S. Patent Office to assist an inventor in establishing the idea or invention as his own. In some respects all three of these procedures do the same thing and if you ever need to prove that an idea or invention belongs to you, you will need all of the paper you can get.

The Record and Disclosure of invention Form should be used when your idea is detailed enough to be understood easily, described and drawn or sketched. It may not be a patentable invention yet but the concept should be clear. I caution you not to wait for full development but to use this form early on. As your invention develops, you can complete additional forms to include and explain details and changes and also show that you have not abandoned the idea but, rather, continued to work on it. It doesn't matter how many times you use this kind of form on the same invention, because, again, you cannot have too much paper when it comes to proving that the idea is yours and that you are continuing to develop it.

Sample Record and Disclosure of Invention Form

What follows is a sample Record and Disclosure of Invention Form. It is not necessary that you use this actual form. Follow the format on plain paper, if you like. You may photocopy the following form and use the copies. Complete the first page using witnesses as previously described. Have your signature notarized with the statement claiming the invention as yours.

On the second page describe your invention using the name of the invention, what the invention is, what it will do, how it should be used and how it could be made including the materials if you know them. Keep it simple. This is not a blueprint; it is a description.

The next page is space for a simple drawing or sketch of the invention. Put is down on paper as best you can. If you have made a model, take pictures and attach them to the form. If it is appropriate, it is a good idea to show the invention from several points of view such as top view, front and side view.

Now that you have completed the form, make at least two copies of it. Use one to work from and one to file in a safe place, away from the place where you work on your invention. That way, if one is destroyed, you will have another available.

Place the original form in a envelope, seal it and mail it to yourself at the Post Office using Certified or Registered Mail. You want a record of the date on which the envelope was mailed. When this "letter" arrives, be sure that no one opens it. Put it in a very safe place. If necessary, you could take the sealed envelope into a court of law and allow it to be opened there. It would be noted that it was brought in sealed, and that it went through the U. S. Post Office on a certain date as shown on the envelope. Therefore, whatever is sealed in the envelope must have been written on or before the date of mailing. It is a good way of confirming the dates on the form, which you have sealed inside. This, along with all of your other paper, will help prove that the invention was yours and that you had been actively working on or developing it.

There are those who will argue the validity of this process. PLEASE UNDERSTAND THAT WHAT I HAVE RECOMMENDED IN THIS BOOK IS ARE METHODS THAT HAVE BEEN USED. I ALSO WANT TO MAKE IT CLEAR THAT NONE OF THESE PROCEEDURES OR ANY COMBINATION OF THEM IS IN ANY WAY A SUBSTITUTE FOR A PATENT, NOR ARE THEY IN AND OF THEMSELVES OR IN ANY COMBINATION A GUARRANTE OF PATENT RIGHTS. The fact is, however that nothing else has been proven more effective. Mr. Gould, the inventor of the LASER is a case in point. The story was written by Rudy Maxa, published in the Washington Post Magazine on February 12, 1978 and shows that without paper of this type he might well have lost his 20 year battle to obtain remuneration for his invention. Paper of this sort can be worth millions. I don't believe that you can have too much of this kind of paper nor do I believe that it can be too carefully or too fully authenticated. Scoffers aside, what does it cost you to take this precaution and what do you stand to loose if you need the paper and don't have it?

ARC HOUSE

RECORD AND DISCLOSURE OF INVENTION

TO WHOM IT MAY CONCERN

BE IT KNOWN THAT _____ Has this _____day of _____, 2000_____ conceived the invention illustrated and described herein this RECORD of INVENTION DOCUMENT, and, further, that the inventor has named and calls the said invention a_____ and has this _____day of _____, 200_____ disclosed to us the following witnesses the details of this invention as known to the inventor which we fully understand the purpose and construction thereof.

Witness_____ Witness_____

State of

_____

County of

_____

I, _____state that I reside at _____ and that I believe myself to be the original, first and sole inventor of the device described herein, and that all dates and statements are true to the best of my knowledge and belief.

Sworn and subscribed before me this _____day of_____, 200_____

Notary Public_____
My commission expires _____

SEAL

DESCRIPTION
OF INVENTION

What to include in your description.
What it is; What it is used for; How it works; How it achieves its purpose; Name of invention; Materials and Mfg. Methods if known.

SKETCH OF INVENTION

Make a simple drawing of sketch of your invention or attach photographs. Show top, front, and side views, if appropriate.

The Disclosure Document Program

The Disclosure Document Program was created by the U. S. Patent Office to provide a form by which the inventor could establish an invention or idea as his own. It is the third type of paper, which I recommend that you use. This form does not in any way substitute for a patent nor does it provide for or in any way guarantee patent rights. Application for a patent is a different and separate`21 process, which you may wish to consider at any point but until you are ready to file for a patent these steps may be helpful in establishing the idea or invention as your own. This form is to be submitted to the U. S. Patent Office in duplicate. The patent office will keep one on file for two years and, if you subsequently apply for a patent, they will include this form in your patent application file. If you do not apply for a patent, the form will be destroyed at the end of the two-year period.

The second copy will be returned to you, usually in a matter of weeks. Place it with your other important papers, You may want to make extra copies so that it can be added to each set of records which you're a re keeping. This form is really just a letter with attachments. You may copy the following.

(Date)

(Your address)

Commissioner of Patents
Washington, D. C. 20231

The undersigned, being the inventor of the disclosed invention, requests that the enclosed papers be accepted under the Disclosure Document Program, and that they be preserved for a period of two years.

Please return the confirming copy with the Disclosure Document Number and the date to the undersigned in the enclosed, self addressed, stamped envelope.

Inventor_____

Co-Inventor (if any)_____

Address_____

City/State_____Zip_____

Enclosures:

    1- Check or money order for filing fee

    2- Description

    3- Sketch, drawing, or photographs

    4- Stamped, self-addressed envelop

You will need to check with the patent office for the current fee. The description and sketch, which are to be enclosed, can be copied right from your latest Record and Disclosure of Invention Form. The stamped, self-addressed envelope should be business size.

Patents

The general term "patent," or more properly "Letters Patent," dates back to the Middle Ages in England where reigning monarchs created monopolies by giving exclusive rights to carry on a specific trade. These rights were meant to give the owner of the patent the benefit of commercializing his invention for a period of time by excluding others from the right to manufacture, use or sell the patented item without the inventor's express permission for which they would pay a fee or royalty.

I recommend that, if you wish to apply for a patent, you contact a Patent Attorney or Patent Agent for guidance. Prior to that, you may want to review the information that is published by the Patent Office. They have several free pamphlets and brochures available that will provide you with information you ought to have before contacting a Patent Attorney or Patent Agent. I believe that this information includes current costs of a patent application but will not include the Patent Attorney or Patent Agent's fee. Also you should know that the patent application fees are expressed as a range. If the initial patent application is not approved the first time, and most are not, you will need to amend the application and apply again. That will add to the costs and there is no guarantee that you will not make several applications before a final decision is rendered.

While many manufacturers want or prefer to see only patented items, others do not. THERE IS NO REQUIREMENT THAT AN ITEM BE PATENTED IN ORDER TO MANUFACTURE AND SELL IT. Personally, I prefer to have a good idea of where and how the item is going to be marketed and by whom before I put money into a patent. I have seen the costs to the inventor rise dramatically by adding the costs of a patent when there is no clear indication that the item will ever be marketed. Sometimes a manufacturer will proceed without a patent. Sometimes an item is marketable but not patentable. Sometimes the manufacturer will pay for the patent. Sometimes the manufacturer will agree to manufacture and market IF the inventor can get the invention patented. I believe in the patent process. I also believe that it is often less necessary than many people would have you think when it comes to marketing. I KNOW THAT patenting in no guarantee that the invention will ever be marketed. I also know of many inventors who have had their invention manufactured at a cost of tens of thousands of dollars but with no marketing guarantee or plan and ended up with a basement full of their product, which no one could sell. Moral: DON'T BET THE FARM.

It is very important to obtain a Preliminary Patent Search in order to determine whether or not you will be likely to infringe upon someone else's already issued patent. The Preliminary Patent results will be the point at which you will decide whether or not to proceed with that particular invention. Such a search can be obtained from a Patent Attorney or a Patent Agent or any reputable firm that offers a Patent Search Service. The Yellow Pages will yield the names of several which you will want to check out as to cost and experience.

Please note that any patent search will only tell you what was patented by the day on which the search was done. The very next day, a patent could be published that would be a duplicate of what you have invented but there will be no indication that it was in process. All patent applications are secret until they are awarded and published. Just because you do not find a precluding patent in a search does not mean that you will have clear sailing to get a patent on your invention.

INVENTOR'S CHECKLIST

1- Prepare your notebook.

2- Consider whom you will ask to be witnesses.

3- Ask them and when they agree, have them witness your entries.

4- When you have developed an idea to the point that it looks like an invention, complete the Record and Disclosure of Invention Form. Have it witnessed and notarized and send a copy to yourself, using Registered or Certified Mail. When it arrives, put it in a save place but DO NOT open it.

5- At the same time, complete the Disclosure Document Program Form and file it with the U.S. Patent Office in duplicate including all of the enclosures.

6- Obtain a preliminary patent search.

7- Consider very carefully whether or not you want to apply for a patent at this time.

Preliminary assessments

Evaluation or engineering report

Now that you have taken the initial steps to establish the idea or invention as yours and have determined from your preliminary patent search that you are going to proceed, you need some factual information from an independent source. The information is called an Evaluation or Engineering Report. It evaluates the invention from several standpoints. Among them are: the description of the invention itself and what it will do. It reviews the productivity of the invention-how it could be manufactured and the techniques required and whether they are readily available. This portion of the report will also comment on the materials needed and their availability. The report should also project production or manufacturer's cost and include estimated wholesale and retail prices. The report should include comments on the market for your invention, how large it is and the likelihood of the market's acceptance of your invention. It should also discuss how the invention could be presented to that market. The costs and market estimates are all just that-estimates but you can at least get an idea of the possibilities. Just don't read them as realities.

Who should do the report?

The purpose of the Evaluation or Engineering Report is to gather information from an impartial source. From it you will determine whether or not you wish to proceed further. Therefore, the information must come from a qualified source in order to lend credibility to your decision and to the information that you will present to manufacturers. This is not a market survey or an overly expansive report. Rather, it is a report of facts (i.e. the invention can be made of tin and soldered together or it can be made of plastic and injection molded. Materials are readily available in the industry.) The projections should be conservative and based on current, accurate information (i.e. currently, according to the last census, there are approximately 70 million households in the U.S. that could use this invention. Typically, about 25% could be expected to buy one over a period of 10 years after it is available on the market.).

Where to find research firms

The Yellow Pages will yield a number of engineering or research firms. If you live in a small town, you may need to use yellow pages from a nearby large city. If you have a friend who has used one and was satisfied, that is a good recommendation. You will need to go through the process of checking out the firm to find out if they can and will do the kind of work you need. Check the cost, time required to do the report and their reputation. If your invention has to do with a particular field, such as electricity, be sure that they have qualified electrical engineers who will not only understand your invention, but who will know how to determine productivity and costs. Be very specific about the report and the information you want. Be very clear about costs. You should be able to get it done for $300.00 to $500.00.

Sign an Invention Disclosure Form

Once you have selected a firm, you may ask them to sign an Invention Disclosure Form for their protection as well as yours. This form will acknowledge that they have received the idea from you, that they have contracted to do work for you on your specific invention, and the invention belongs entirely to you. A sample form is on the following page.

INVENTION DISCLOSURE FORM

To whom it may concern:

Be it known that _____

Has on this _____ day of _____, 200___, disclosed the details of an

Invention called _____

to_____

of (company name)_____

(address)_____

The purpose of this disclosure is _____

_____

_____

_____

The work contracted for hereunder is expected to be completed by _____

_____at a cost of_____.

It is agreed and understood that disclosure to the above named person constitutes disclosure to all company personnel, and it is acknowledged that the invention named herein does belong to _____in its entirety, including any variations or improvements which may be discovered as a result of the work done under this agreement. Further, the contracting company agrees to take all reasonable precaution to protect the secrecy of this invention and all variations.

_____   Date_____
Signature of company representative

_____   Date_____
Signature of inventor

Models

The primary purpose of building any kind of model is to reduce the theory of the invention to practice. It is not mandatory that you provide a model. The Patent Office no longer accepts models and a manufacturer may or may not want to see one. It is acceptable to tell a manufacturer that no model or prototype exists. Your case may be much stronger if you can tell a manufacturer that you have tested a working model and can answer questions from that perspective.

Sometimes it is not practical to build a working model. It may be too expensive or it may take equipment, which you do not have. A good example would be the laser, designed by Mr. Gould. A misunderstanding about the need for a model stopped him from presenting his idea to manufacturers. When you do not build a model, there should be a good reason.

Three Types of Models

In considering whether to build a model, you need to know what type of model to build. That will depend on what you want the model to do. A model, to show what it looks like; a working model, to show how it functions; or a prototype from which it will be manufactured. Each of these three types of models performs a role in the development, manufacturing and marketing of your invention. See the glossary for a more complete definition of each type. The manufacturer, for instance, usually builds the prototype, during preparation for production. A working model is most likely what you will need.

INVENTOR'S CHECKLIST

1-Choose a company from whom you will obtain an Evaluation or Engineering Report.

2-Sign an Invention Disclosure Form.

3-Build a model of the invention.

Part III-PRESENTING YOUR IDEA TO THE MANUFACTURER

Arnold Keith Winkelman

Marketing your invention

Manufacturers are always looking for new products from which to make a profit. They might be interested in your idea provided it is new, marketable, not already on their drawing boards, is easily producible, and, most of all, will attract a market and make a profit. You must also show that it belongs to you and, therefore, that you have something to sell, that is you have the right to sell the idea or license the manufacturer to produce and market your idea. You need to show that it can be produced with relative ease using existing technology and readily available material or that the profit will be worth the cost of whatever it takes to produce the product. You will need to convince the manufacturer that a market exists for the product, a market that is not already being served or show why your idea would result in a better product that that market would accept. It may be necessary to show that the market is large enough so that your product would be profitable by capturing a reasonable percentage due to your improvements or superiority. Your invention must show that it has the potential of turning a profit high enough to make the risk of production worthwhile. Just as your invention involved listening, finding a need, and fulfilling that need, now you must do the same with a manufacturer. You will have to sell your idea to the manufacturer with fact and figures, not high pressure. The ability to sell is so important to your success that you may need a professional to do it for you, but first let's see how you could go about presenting your idea to a manufacturer.

All ideas, inventions, or products should be presented to qualified manufacturers on paper since more than one person will usually be involved in making the decision to accept or reject your idea. The manufacturer's first decision will be whether or not to even consider your idea so the paper you present is crucial.

Remember, the manufacturer did not ask you to submit your idea. The manufacturer is under no obligation to even look at your presentation or give it serious consideration. Courtesy says he will, but he is under no obligation. That means that you must not waste his time. Provide a complete concept and present it in a simple form. You are not writing a commercial. Your goal is to get the manufacturer to consider your idea as a product which he can and should produce, one that will make money for him.

New Product Submission Form

What follows is a New Product Submission Form. Change it as you wish but this form does the job well. It was created from researching manufacturers to find out what kind of information they want and how they want it presented. Your only purpose is to get the manufacturer's attention and interest. A manufacturer will not take the time to wade through a lot of disorganized material to come to an understanding of the idea or invention. Be clear, be succinct and brief, but complete.

NEW PRODUCT SUBMISSION

INVENTION SUBMITTED BY_____

Address_____

CITY/STATE/ZIP_____

NAME OF INVENTOR_____
    PLEASE SEND ALL CORRESPONDENCE TO THIS ADDRESS USING FILE # NOTED BELOW
NAME OF INVENTION _____FILE # _____

BRIEF DESCRIPTION_____

_____

_____

TO:_____ATT:_____

    The following is a description of an excellent idea, which we believe lies within your capabilities and interests as a addition to your product line, or as a possible area of diversification. The new Product Submission is intended to include enough information to guide you in making a decision as to the extent of your interest in the described invention.

    We would be receptive to licensing by your firm not only to manufacture but also to market and distribute and will safeguard your right through a written agreement.

    If you are not in a position to manufacture this item yourselves, you may have sources from which you would like to procure it. We will be happy to work through a third firm to get this product into your domain. If you are interested in this item as a proprietary product, but do not wish to get involved in any of the manufacturing or procurement process, We will be pleased to seek and negotiate with a competent supplier in your behalf.

    This presentation and the disclosures herein are made voluntarily. Should your firm desire to explore licensing or acquisition of this invention, we will then expect confidential treatment of ensuing negotiations by all concerned.

    We will look forward to hearing from you soon and will appreciate being notified even if your company's reaction is not a positive one.

Date_____   Inventor_____

DESCRIPTION:

AVAILABLE MODELS:

PRODUCIBILITY:

FEATURES:

ADVANTAGES:

MARKETS:

COST DATA:

PATENT STATUS:

BELOW IS A SIMPLE SKETCH OR PHOTOGRAPH OF A MODEL

ATTACHED IS A COPY OF A LETTER SUMMARIZING THE PATENT SEARCH

CHOOSING THE LIST OF MANUFACTURERS

There are several ways to find manufacturers who are capable of producing your invention. The main problem is in finding manufacturers who are interested at this time and who are willing to accept ideas for new products from outside their own company or outside their own research and development departments. For the individual inventor, it is mostly trial and error because there is nothing published which will list the manufactures that are open to receiving unsolicited ideas. Often, acceptance will depend on such factors as the current economy, the manufacturers own line of products and the current management attitude. Your trial and error method should begin in the Reference Section of your local library with THE THOMAS REGISTER. If you are not familiar with it, you will need to learn how to use it. Your Reference Librarian will assist you.

After you have categorized your item and made your initial list of manufacturers to contact, go to stores and look for similar items. Maybe the similarity is "plastic" or "battery operated" or "household items." Think in terms of similar materials and manufacturing techniques. Be creative. Write down the name and address of any manufacturers that you find this way and add them to your list.

If your item can be made in a foreign country where production costs are lower than in the United Stated, either the embassy for that country or a trade association promoting that country's interest will be glad to supply you with names and addresses of manufacturers.

CAUTION: When dealing with foreign manufacturers, you protection is limited, perhaps even non-existent. There is no such thing as a universal or international patent. You may have heard about the extension of certain rights in certain, but not all, countries. This extension of rights is not patent protection in the fullest sense. Even so, you don't want the hassle of a lawsuit in a foreign country. I'm not saying don't do it, I am saying be careful.

If you have the opportunity to attend a trade show, which includes your type of item, do so and be sure to pick up a catalog. It will include the names and addresses of manufacturers, distributors and the like.

Trade magazines and advertising will also give you names of manufacturers. You can often find trade magazines in your local library.

One way to overcome some of the problems is to hire a professional to do the presentation for you. A good professional marketing consultant or firm should be able to write the presentation well and give you a good list of manufacturers. It won't be perfect, and even the professional cannot promise success. Check them out carefully and be sure that they have had success with other items in the same category as your invention.

In addition to the Thomas Register, you may want to use some of the following:

HOW TO FIND INFORMATION ABOUT COMPANIES
DIRECTORY OF AMERICAN FIRMS OPERATING IN FOREIGN COUNTRIES
DIRECTORY OF FOREIGN MANUFACTURERS IN THE UNITED STATES
CORPORATE AFFILIATIONS
MILLION DOLLAR DIRECTORY
MOODY'S INDUSTRIAL MANUAL
TOY AND HOBBY WORLD

Keep a record

However you choose to do so, keep a record. Always keep a record. Your record should include a copy of every piece of paper that you send out, the date it was sent, any follow-up, notes about any telephone conversation including the date, with whom you spoke, what was said, and the results of your effort. You need to know the status with any manufacturer to whom you have made a submission. If you sign, not just agree to verbally, a licensing agreement, you will need to let any manufacturers who have outstanding submissions know that your item is no longer available. Don't explain why or to whom you have licensed it, just inform them that it is no longer available.

Responses: How long does it take?

Responses from manufacturers take time. Do not expect many responses in less than thirty (30) to sixty (60) days. It may take much longer. Manufacturers are under no obligation to answer at all. After sixty (60) days have gone by with no response from the manufacturer, you should follow up by inquiring as to whether or not they received your New Product Submission. You may want to include a copy. If you do not get a response from the follow-up, you can probably mark that one off.

A positive response

By a positive response, I mean a response from the manufacturer that states that the manufacturer is interested in your invention. A request that the manufacturer wants you to sign their disclosure form before they will consider the invention further is not necessarily a positive response. However, you will need to sign their disclosure form and return it to get them to make a decision as to the extent of their interest.

Interest is expressed, the manufacturer will ask for further information from you. Frequently, it will appear that the manufacturer is asking for information that was already provided in the submission. What the manufacturer usually means is that they want more in-depth information on the same subject. For instance, if you are asked if a working model or prototype is available when you have already stated that it was, the manufacturer probably wants to know more about the size, what materials you used and whether or not it could be sent to his plant to look at.

If you do not understand what the manufacturer wants, ask him directly. Call the person who wrote the letter and get a clear understanding. If you have no additional information, say so and see if that leads you to another area of negotiation. You may be able to obtain the information that the manufacturer is requesting or you can explain why you can't. Keep the discussion alive. It will move you toward a positive resolve.

The <u>Licensing</u> <u>Agreement</u>

When all of the questions about the invention have been answered and the manufacturer is interested in acquiring the rights to your invention, you will be asked about a Licensing Agreement. The manufacturer may send you a copy of his standard form, or he may simply ask you what kind of an agreement and how much royalty you are expecting. If the manufacturer sends a copy of his agreement, compare it to yours or the one that follows in this book. At this point, you may wish to enlist legal help to be sure that you ask for everything you should have in a Licensing Agreement that is designed for your invention. When your attorney advises, send the manufacturer a copy of the Licensing Agreement that you want and explain why your want it written this way. Leave plenty of room for negotiation in your requests but make you statements assertive and clear.

A Licensing Agreement is the instrument used to give a manufacturer permission to produce and sell your invention. For that privilege, the manufacturer pays a royalty.

A Licensing Agreement is also a contract. All contracts have three basic parts: offer, acceptance and consideration. After that it gets a little more complicated. Basically, the manufacturer offers to manufacture (or manufacture, distribute, and sell but be sure that it is clear what the manufacturer is offering to do and within what kind of a time frame) your invention. You accept the manufacturer's offer. The consideration is the amount of money used to seal the contract and includes the royalty that the manufacturer is going to pay you. It may also include the cost of molds, applying for and obtaining a patent and other expenses that must be spelled out in the agreement. It may be that you, the inventor, may agree to apply for a patent and pay all of the associated costs.

Other considerations may include:

The quantity that the manufacturer will produce and sell annually.

The date that production will begin.

The date that the manufacturer will begin paying royalty.

The price on which the royalty will be paid. Will it be the manufacturer's cost, billed price, number produced, or number sold?

How long will the agreement last? Will it be automatically renewable? Does either party have the right to decline automatic renewal?

What if the manufacturer goes bankrupt? What will happen to the rights, the molds, and the inventory?

Who will fund and own the patent?

In order to answer these questions, a sample Licensing Agreement follows. Read through it carefully.

Licensing Agreement

This Agreement, made this _____ day of _____, 200____,

By and between_____

Hereinafter referred to as MANUFACTURER and _____

hereinafter referred to as LICENSOR.

Whereas, Licensor represents and warrants that he is the sole owner of all rights, titles

and interests to a device named _____, and

Whereas, Manufacturer is desirous of acquiring an exclusive license to manufacture,

distribute, sell and use said device under the terms and conditions hereinafter set forth;

Now Therefore, the said parties in consideration of the mutual covenants and

agreements contained herein and in further consideration of the sum of

$_____ do agree as follows:

1. Licensor hereby grants to Manufacturer the sole and exclusive license to manufacture, distribute, sell and use said device in all foreign and domestic markets legally available anywhere in the world throughout the life of this agreement within the terms and conditions hereinafter stated.

2. The life of this agreement shall be for _____ years. Subject to the agreement of all parties concerned an option for automatic renewal is provided. Such renewal option shall be automatic unless notice to the contrary is given in writing not less than thirty (30) days prior to the expiration of this agreement.

3. It is recognized by both parties hereto that Manufacturer will require a Certain length of time to work out production and sales strategy and, Therefore, no minimum requirement or production shall be effective Between the date of this agreement and the production date of the 1st day of _____, 200____. However, Manufacturer agrees to expedite production and sales as

much as possible and to pay full royalty as provided herein on all said devices sold during this period.

4. Manufacturer agrees to pay Licensor a royalty of _____ on each and every said device sold. Said royalty to be due and payable at the end of each there month period following the aforementioned production date and shall be transferred not later than the 15th of the month following the end of each three month period.

5. Manufacturer agrees to pay to Licensor or Licensor's agents or Assigns the aforementioned percentage of royalty on a minimum of_____ dollars worth of sales or _____ devices produced whether or not those amounts are actually sold or produced. Maximum payment is to be based on the actual number of said devices. Sold or actual dollars worth of sales made whether payment has been collected or not. Failure of Manufacturer to pay the aforementioned royalty on the above stated minimum shall give Licensor or it's agents or assigns the right to terminate this agreement at it's option.

6. Manufacturer shall affix or cause to be affixed to each said device or to the container in which said device may be sold the inscription "Patent No._____" or "Patent applied for" if applicable.

7. Manufacturer shall at all times keep true and correct records of accounts showing the total number of said devices produced and sold and these accounts shall be open to inspection by Licensor, it's agents or assigns at all usual and proper business times and Manufacturer shall render a full statement of net sales (sales minus returns) made at the end of each three month period.

8. It is agreed that if royalties (meaning any part thereof) shall at any time be in arrears, or if Manufacturer shall become bankrupt, insolvent, or enter into any composition with its' creditors, or shall make any default in performing any of the agreements contained herein, then it shall be lawful for Licensor, its agents or assigns, by written notice sent by registered mail to the Manufacturer's last known address, to revoke this agreement which shall become void without prejudice to any right of action or remedy of Licensor for the recovery of any monies then due. Such notice shall provide thirty (30) days for reinstatement of

this agreement provided manufacturer corrects the fault and shows his ability to comply in the future.

9. Manufacturer shall have the right to grant sub-licenses to other Manufacturers under the same terms and conditions and royalty payments to Licensor as herein contained.

10. Manufacturer further agrees that it will diligently pursue the Manufacture and sale of said devices during the life of this agreement and will exert its best efforts toward creating and fulfilling the demand thereof.

11. If, at any time hereafter, during the continuance of this Agreement, Licensor, it's agents or assigns, shall make any improvement in said device, then such improvement shall inure to the benefit of manufacturer without any addition to the royalty percentage stipulated herein. Conversely, any improvement to said device made by Manufacturer shall inure to the benefit of Licensor, it's agents or assigns, under the terms and agreements including royalty payments as stated herein.

12. Manufacturer agrees that it will not, during the term of this agreement, directly or indirectly attack or question the validity of any protection imposed on said device.

13. In the event that said device should be infringed upon, or appear to be an infringement upon, then the manufacturer or the Licensor, whoever discovers the apparent infringement, must notify the other as soon as possible. After notification, the manufacturer may at its election prosecute such possible infringement at its own expense and retain any monies awarded in settlement. However, if Manufacture elects not to prosecute, then Licensor, its agents or assigns, may elect to do so at its own expense and retain any monies awarded in settlement.

14. This agreement shall not be transferable by the Manufacturer except with the written consent of Licensor and shall be binding upon all agents and assigns of either.

15. The manufacturer shall indemnify and save the Licensor totally harmless from any and all claims, actual or alleged, arising out of the manufacturing,

production, distribution or sale of the product named herein whether such claim arises from the manufacturer, the manufacturer's employees, contractors, agents or any purchaser.

16. This agreement is considered and understood to be binding for it's full term and all renewals on both the Manufacturer and the Licensor and shall continue to apply to the legal representatives, heirs, agents or assigns of either.

17. Any notices required to be given under this agreement shall be sent by certified mail through the U. S. Post Office, postage prepaid, to the last known address set forth in this agreement.

18. The royalty to be paid to the Licensor by the Manufacturer, as stated in paragraph 4, is further described as the agreed upon percentage of the net sales which are herein described and defined as being the total consideration received by the manufacturer for the product sold without deducting any cost of doing business including but not limited to the costs of raw materials, processing, packaging, shipping, sales advertising, commissions, overhead or other expenses or costs usual to production, manufacturing, distribution or sales. Net sales, billed price, or total consideration received will generally be computed by multiplying the list price of the product times the total number of the product sold deducting there from the discounts allowed to distributors and wholesalers, cash discounts, credits for returns and allowances for defective or damaged products.

19. In order for the Manufacturer to make at least one prototype, determine his own production costs and survey his own markets, the Licensor does grant to the Manufacturer an option of _____ days from the date of this agreement. During this option period, the manufacturer may cancel this agreement and forfeit all rights as herein described.

The manufacturer agrees to submit to the Licensor all changes proposed and/or incorporated as soon as practical and does agree to keep Licensor informed and up to date as to the changes and progress of the production for any and all models or prototypes.

Should the Manufacturer desire to proceed with this agreement after the option period, Manufacturer will mail notice to the Licensor by the last day of the option and will include the payment of $_____

as the initial consideration for this licensing agreement.

20. Any and all notices required under this agreement are to be mailed through the U. S. Post Office by certified mail, postage prepaid.

The addresses for notices are as follows:

For the Manufacturer:

For the Licensor:

In Witness Whereof, Manufacturer and Licensor have hereunto executed this agreement in each individual name by its proper officer who is duly authorized and each has hereunto affixed its seal.

Manufacturer:

_____

By: _____Date_____

Licensor:

_____

By:_____Date_____

INVENTOR'S CHECKLIST

1- Complete the New Product Submission Form.

2- Choose a list of manufacturers to contact.

3- Keep an ongoing record of all submissions sent, telephone calls, correspondence, questions, answers – a complete record of everything that happens pertaining to your invention.

4- Wait for a response.

5- Negotiate a Licensing Agreement.

GLOSSARY

Claims - In the body of a patent, the statements of what is claimed to be new and useful.

Copyright - A way to protect literary, dramatic, musical and artistic works.

Design Patent - A patent issued on the new, useful and unique design or configuration of an item.

Disclosure - The telling or allowing others than the inventor to know about, as in the Disclosure of Invention Form.

Disclosure Document Program - A way of establishing an idea or invention as Belonging to an inventor. The program was established by the U. S. Patent Office.

Drawing or Sketch - The simple picture of the invention on paper, without much detail. A simple picture which shows what the invention will look like or what the Inventor had in mind.

Evaluation - A report, usually made at least in part by an Engineer knowledgable in the Field, which provides the inventor with impartial information about his invention regarding the manufacturing process to be used, materials, costs, packaging, markets, functionality – an overall feasibility study of the manufacturing and marketing of the invention.

Field of Search - The classes and subclasses of patents, which the searcher reviewed in making the patent search. The categories of patents found at the U. S. Patent Office.

Hold harmless - To take the liability of another. In this context, to pay for the harm an invention has caused, thereby taking the liability of the inventor and holding him without a loss.

Improvement - As used in this context, a change in the invention which makes the invention better than it was, or different, or even makes it into another invention.

Invention - A new and useful item. The parts may not be new, but the combination must produce something new and useful and different from the sum of its parts.

Inventor - On who creates a new and useful item.

Inventor's Notebook - A bound notebook into which pages cannot be inserted that is used by an inventor to record his thoughts and ideas as he invents and to establish them as belonging to the inventor.

Licensee - One who is licensed to manufacture, produce, distribute and/or sell an invention.

Licensing Agreement - A contract giving permission to produce, manufacture, distribute and/or sell the invention in return for a price or royalty or other consideration to be paid to the inventor.

Licensor - One who grants a license (i.e. the inventor).

Manufacturer - One who makes or produces items. Here is meant to be a manufacturer who is large enough to make, distribute, and sell the invention in question and/or a manufacturer who is licensed to do so.

Marketing - The selling of anything. In this context, the selling of an invention to a manufacturer or selling the manufactured invention to the public.

Marketplace - Generally, the retail marketplace, where products are sold such stores, shops, catalogs and the like. It is also used to mean the place where inventions are sold to manufacturers.

Mechanical or Utility Patent - A patent issued on a mechanical device as opposed to a design or plant.

Model - A likeness of the invention (not necessarily a working likeness).

Notary Public - A person licensed to witness signatures and sworn statements.

Option period - A time when the manufacturer can try out the idea of producing the invention and accept the license or decline it without penalty.

Patent - A paper, issued by a government, granting certain rights to an inventor for a particular invention, all for a specified period of time.

Patent Attorney - An attorney who specializes in patent law and patent procedures and who is admitted to practice in a patent court.

Patent Examiner - A person who examines applications for patents, searches the U. S. Patent Office records, foreign patent records, printed publications, and his own collection of files in order to determine whether or not a patent will be issued.

Patent number - The number of an issued patent, which must appear on each item produced under that patent.

Patent Record Review - The report made by the patent searcher on a particular invention, the report following a patent search.

Patent Search - Any of a variety of searches through the records of the U. S. Patent Office.

Plant Patent - A patent issued on a particular plant.

Preliminary Patent Search - The first patent search, usually a search of less depth than Later searches done to determine patentability.

Prototype - A working model that is actually a pattern from which all copies will be made and sold.

Record and Disclosure of Invention Form - A form used to record and disclose an invention, It is witnessed and contains a description and sketches of the invention.

References - The patents, which are found to be similar in some, respect or found to be close to the invention on which a patent search is made.

Royalty - The consideration paid for the license (of an invention).

Trademark - A mark used to identify a product or company.

Witness - One who can attest to what he has seen, read or heard about the invention (from the inventor).

Working Model - A likeness of the invention, which demonstrates how it functions.

ABOUT THE AUTHOR

Mr. Winkelman has consulted with hundred of inventors and shown them the way to transfer the idea in their head into an effective, organized and protected presentation to manufacturers who have the capability of getting your invention on the market. Here it is in a book that will guide you through the process step by step.